English FOR YOUR Success

W9-AUE-355

A Language Development Program for African American Children

Curriculum Guide for Grades 2-3

Los Angeles Unified School District

Noma LeMoine

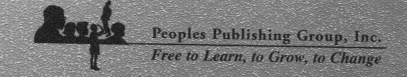
Peoples Publishing Group, Inc.
Free to Learn, to Grow, to Change

Credits

Project Manager, Eric Grajo
Copy Editor, Christine Cannistraro
Cover Design, Jeremy Mayes
Design, Doreen Smith, Eric Grajo, Jennifer Bridges
Production/Electronic Design, Eric Grajo, Jennifer Bridges

Credits

Special thanks to Robert Siller for providing definitions for African Symbols, page 20, © copyright 1934 by Lillian M. Bowles Music, Published by National Baptist Publishing Board; page 21, permission granted by UPI/Corbis-Bettmann; page 27, © copyright (William Morrow, 1991), (Quill/William Morrow, 1995), Clip Art by Corel Draw
Cover Illustration by Doris Hughes

Instructional Advisor for Curriculum Guide 2-3:

Anthony Jackson

Peoples Publishing Group, Inc.
Free to Learn, to Grow, to Change

© 1999 The Peoples Publishing Group
230 West Passaic Street
Maywood, New Jersey 07607

All rights reserved. No part of this book may be kept in an information storage or retrieval system, transmitted or reproduced in any form or by any means without prior written permission of the Publisher.

ALL COPYING PROHIBITED BY LAW UNLESS GRANTED BY PUBLISHER OR NOTED ON SPECIFIC PAGES IN THIS PUBLICATION.

Printed in the United States of America
10 9 8 7 6 5 4 3 2 1

ISBN 1 - 56256 - 446-3

African symbols used throughout the book

 This symbol originated in Northern Nigeria and was created to look like a relief design on a mud wall.

 This symbol originated in Kinshasha, Congo, and was created to decorate cloth.

 This symbol originated in Benin, Nigeria, and was created to look like a carved wood pattern.

 This symbol originated in the Kinshasha, Congo, and was created to look like a design on a wooden basket.

 This symbol originated in Northern Senegal and was created to decorate cloth.

 This symbol comes from Congo, Kinshasha, and was created to look like a Bangba painted wall design.

 This symbol comes from Bida, Nigeria, and was created to look like a mud wall design.

 This symbol originated in Ghana and was created to look like an Ashanti bronze gold weight.

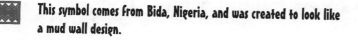 This symbol originated in the Congo, Kinshasha, and was created to look like a Bushongo woven wall matting design.

This symbol comes from Ghana and was created to look like an Ashanti bronze box design.

 This symbol originated in Congo, Kinshasha, and was created to look like a carved pattern on a Bushongo wooden drum.

 This symbol originated in Northern Nigeria and was created to look like a mud wall relief design.

 This symbol originated in Eastern Nigeria and was created to look like an Igbo painted wall pattern.

 This symbol originated in Benin, Nigeria, and was created to look like a bronze sculpture design.

 This symbol originated in Ghana and was created to look like an Ashanti "Adinkira" printing stamp pattern.

 This symbol originated in Western Nigeria and was created to look like a carved pattern on a Yoruba ivory Jug.

 This symbol originated in South Africa and was created to look like a Zulu wood carving.

This symbol originated in South Africa and was created to look like a common Tsonga pottery motif.

This symbol originated in Cameroon and was created to look like a beadwork design on a Bali Calabash cover.

This symbol originated in Northern Senegal and was created to look like decorated cloth.

Peoples Publishing Group, Inc.   Copying Prohibited by Law   1-800-822-1080

English For Your Success

Curriculum Guide for Grades 2-3

Table of Contents

English For Your Success

Curriculum Guide for Grades 2-3

Table of Contents
Continued

INTRODUCTION

English for Your Success was created and refined in the Los Angeles Unified School District over a six-year period by Noma LeMoine as Director of the project, and with the contributions of many educators within the district. This language development program for African American learners has been successful, and The Peoples Publishing Group is happy to publish it to share with you.

The program revolves around the **Handbook of Successful Strategies for Teachers**, a combination teacher's edition and training manual for this program. Before using this Curriculum Guide, you will want to have your own copy of the Handbook to review. **English for Your Success** is organized around twelve instructional goals:

1. acquiring an awareness and appreciation of home language and culture.
2. developing receptive language in Mainstream American English.
3. acquiring basic literacy skills.
4. developing an awareness and appreciation of language and cultural diversity.
5. being able to recognize and label the differences between African American Language and Mainstream American English.
6. expanding a personal thesaurus of conceptually coded word concepts.
7. analyzing linguistic differences between Mainstream American English and African American Language.
8. using Mainstream American English structure functionally in oral and written form.
9. recognizing the language requirements of different situations.
10. demonstrating proficient use of Mainstream American English in written and oral form.
11. developing an expanded knowledge and appreciation of African American Language and the languages and cultures of others.
12. communicating effectively in cross-cultural environments.

This Curriculum Guide for Grades two through three has eight complete lessons to use with your students—two lessons for each of the first eight instructional goals which are grade-level appropriate for Grades 2-3. We hope that you and your pupils enjoy and learn from these model lessons. We also encourage you to take the next step of writing your own lessons for appropriate instructional goals using books and information you select for your pupils. To aid you in writing your own lessons, we have provided a Lesson Organizer for you at the back of this book. Please copy it and use it to organize your lessons for your own classroom.

We wish you success with **English for Your Success**.

Instructional Goals for Grades 2-3

Acquiring an awareness and appreciation of home language and culture

Developing receptive language in Mainstream American English (MAE)

Acquiring basic literacy skills

Developing an awareness and appreciation of language and cultural diversity

Being able to recognize and label the differences between African American Language (AAL) and Mainstream American English (MAE)

Expanding a personal thesaurus of conceptually coded word concepts

Analyzing linguistic differences between Mainstream American English (MAE) and African American Language (AAL)

Using Mainstream American English (MAE) structure functionally in oral and written form

THE BEST FACE OF ALL
by Wilesse A.F. Commissiong
Illustrated by Buck Brown

GOAL

Using the book *The Best Face of All*, pupils will:

acquire an awareness and appreciation of **home language and culture** by:

- using **literature that reflects the pupils home life**, personal interest, cultural background and language,
- creating a **print-rich classroom** emphasizing **small group activities** with cooperative and mediated learning to encourage language development and the sharing of ideas and learning strategies.

MATERIALS **TO PREPARE**

for each pupil in the group,

- a copy of *The Best Face of All*, if possible. If not, use one copy with the group
- **pictures** of a wide variety of different children, all colors and looks, including handicapped, those with eyeglasses, braces, etc. and all different hair styles, engaging in a variety of activities, including both physically active and intellectually active
- Try to reflect the physical makeup of your classroom and school

to use with the group

- **chalkboard** or **class chart** available for use

Materials to Prepare **for Cross Curricular Links**

LANGUAGE ARTS paper

SCIENCE class chart or lined paper to make a chart

ART crayons, including people or skin-colored crayons, paper suitable for coloring with crayons, lined writing paper, safety scissors, non-toxic glue

COOPERATIVE LEARNING lined writing paper

PARENTAL INVOLVEMENT copies of *The Best Face of All* for pupils to take home

PART 1 INTO the Lesson

INTRODUCTION

Introduce the concept of best.

What does being the best mean?
Can you have only one best, or can there be many different bests?
Each of us has some best skills or qualities.
What are some of your best qualities?

Encourage each pupil to be honest and realistic, but to identify some positive quality of theirs to reinforce. Reinforce internal qualities more than external qualities such as prettiness or attractive features. Focus pupils on the internal as more important. Be sure that each pupil is described positively in some aspect.

Everyone has some best, special qualities. Everyone deserves respect. What does respect mean?

Encourage pupils to focus on respecting all people by being polite, listening, sharing, and not hurting others. Encourage discussion of other ways to show respect.

What about the way we look?
Can people be unfair or disrespectful about the way a person looks?
Does that hurt people?
Is it respectful?

Discuss the importance of respecting and appreciating physical differences.

There are many different bests, many different types of beauty, inside and outside. It's fun to be different and to look different, isn't it? Each of you is beautiful in a different way. Isn't it fun to work on your own special beauty and enjoy it? How do you feel when you treat others badly? When you treat them with respect?

Encourage discussion of differences and what fun that is, and of what we learn from others.

PREREADING

Do not give each pupil a book yet. Instead, show pupils the covers (front and back) of the book and the title page. Have pupils read the name of the book, the author, and the illustrator.

Now tell pupils to watch quietly, not talking, as you show them some pages from the inside of the book.

What do you think the story is about?

You may wish to record pupils' predictions on the chalkboard or class chart for review after reading the story.

Is there a best face of all?
Is one color better than another?
Is there one kind of hair that's better than another?
Are girls better than boys? Boys better than girls?

Display pictures of a variety of people representing a variety of colors, looks, and doing a variety of tasks. Encourage pupils to understand that people are all different colors and shapes and skills, but that each person and group deserves respect.

PART 2 THROUGH the Lesson

GUIDED READING

If you have enough copies of the book, distribute them to individual pupils now. Begin by reading the story aloud and having pupils help you while using the class chart to record phrases for choral reading, e.g.

Which eyes are best?
Which noses are best?
Which is the best hair of all?

Have pupils answer each question collectively as a group with, e.g. My eyes are best while pointing to their own eyes, or All of our eyes are best! You may wish to write pupils' answers to the questions on the class chart or chalkboard.

Next, reread the story having individual pupils read aloud. Encourage choral reading of sentences pupils picked out for the class chart. Stop and explain any vocabulary words with which pupils have difficulty. Discuss the story to ensure that pupils understand that each of us has the best face and that all faces are best.

You may wish to have pupils reread the story silently instead.

Review pupils' predictions and discuss where they matched or did not match what the story was about.

Copying Prohibited by Law
The Best Face of All

PART 3 BEYOND the Lesson

CROSS CURRICULAR LINKS

LANGUAGE ARTS

Have pupils work individually or in pairs to create diamantes, or poems in the shape of a diamond, to describe themselves. Then, have pupils share their diamantes. Here are two examples of diamantes by a girl named Kiesha Washington. You may wish to copy them onto the chalkboard or class chart. Encourage pupils to write two different diamantes—one that describes physical beauty and one that describes their inner beauty.

Kiesha
long fingers
soft full arms
ebony warm smooth face
long round legs
brown eyes
Washington

Kiesha
Kind Loving
Joyful Patient Giving
Funny Laughing Sensitive Quiet
Friendly Sharing Happy
Wonderful Cheery
Washington

You may wish to have pupils read and discuss other books on appreciation and respect for self and others differences. Here are some suggestions.

A is for Africa by Ifeonma Onyefulu
All the Colors of the Earth by Sheila Hamanaka
All the Colors of the Race by Arnold Adoff
Colors Around Me by Vivian Church
Come With Me to Africa by Gregory Scott Kreikemeier
I'm Glad I'm Me by Elberta H. Stone
The Tiger Who Wore White Gloves by Gwendolyn Brooks
Brown Angels: An Album of Pictures and Verse by Walter Dean Myers
Brown Honey in Broomwheat Tea by Joyce Carol Thomas
Honey, I Love by Eloise Greenfield
Soul Looks Back in Wonder by Tom Feelings

Here are some suggestions for books on friendship.

Imani's Gift at Kwanzaa by Deborah Newton Chocolate
Me and Neesie by Eloise Greenfield
Meet Danitra Brown by Nikki Grimes

CROSS CURRICULAR LINKS

SCIENCE

Help pupils hypothesize about why different people have different hair texture and color, skin color, and eye color. Where do pupils get their physical characteristics? Help pupils make genetics charts listing the hair color, texture, skin color, and eye color of their parents, and their own. Explain that some physical characteristics are inherited as genes. (Note: do not distinguish between pupils who know their biological parents and those who do not. Simply help pupils conclude that often, although not always, these physical characteristics are inherited. If not from their parents, then they may be inherited from grandparents, etc.)

ART

Have each pupil draw and cut out two paper dolls representing themselves, coloring them with their own skin color, eye color, etc. Have each pupil write one diamante on a doll, and display the dolls. Help pupils as needed to write their diamantes on their dolls. It may be easier for pupils to write their diamantes on lined paper, cut them out, and glue them onto the dolls.

You may wish to research and show pupils examples of other poetic forms, e.g. haiku, and have them write self-descriptive poems in those forms.

COOPERATIVE LEARNING

In groups, have pupils discuss new ways to make friends. Have each group make a list and share it with the class.

PARENTAL INVOLVEMENT

Encourage pupils to take home a copy of *The Best Face of All* to read and discuss with parents.

IMANI'S GIFT AT KWANZAA

by Denise Burden-Patmon
Illustrated by Floyd Cooper

NOTE: Since this is a Kwanzaa lesson, you may want to use it at Kwanzaa time. Since pupils should do research in this lesson, you should have one or more of the following resources available to them:

Kwanzaa by Deborah M. Newton Chocolate
Kwanzaa by A.P. Porter
Have a Happy... by Mildred Pitts Walter
My First Kwanzaa Book by Deborah M. Newton Chocolate

GOAL

Using the book *Imani's Gift at Kwanzaa,* pupils will:
demonstrate an awareness and appreciation of **home language and culture** by:
▨▨▨ learning about **Kwanzaa.**

MATERIALS TO PREPARE

for each pupil in the group,
◉ if possible, a copy of the book *Imani's Gift at Kwanzaa*
◉ copy of the **copy master** at the end of this lesson
◉ **lined paper**

to use with the group,
▨▨▨ at least one copy of the book *Imani's Gift at Kwanzaa*
▨▨▨ **chalkboard** or **class chart**

Materials to Prepare for Cross Curricular Links

LANGUAGE ARTS the books listed above as resources to research Kwanzaa, paper, and art materials to make and illustrate pupils' own books

LANGUAGES-SWAHILI one or more of the following books that teach Swahili words:
Imani's Gift at Kwanzza (Glossary) by Denise Burden-Patmon
Jambo Means Hello by Tom Feelings
Moja Means One by Tom Feelings

MATHEMATICS list of Swahili numbers, one through ten, paper
ART materials identified by pupils to create *zawadi*, e.g. beads and strings, and art materials

MUSIC Pupils will need time to find African recordings that they like and that you wish to use in the classroom.

PART 1 INTO the Lesson

INTRODUCTION

Do you know what Kwanzaa is?

Explain to pupils that it is an African American holiday created by Dr. Maulana Karenga. African Americans and many of African descent celebrate Kwanzaa to reunite and celebrate the special qualities of African cultures. Kwanzaa is not a religious holiday, although many churches celebrate it in a religious fashion.

Chalkboard

Using the class chart or chalkboard, have pupils list their questions about Kwanzaa. Pupils will use these questions in cooperative learning groups to research the books and find answers.

Be sure that, in their research, pupils find out the seven principles of Nguzo Saba (in GOO zoh SAH bah) upon which Kwanzaa is based. (These are listed on a copy master at the end of this lesson.)

On the class chart or chalkboard, list the answers to pupils' questions. Discuss what pupils have learned about Kwanzaa.

PREREADING

Introduce the book *Imani's Gift at Kwanzaa* to the pupils.

We will read a story together. It is about a little girl named Imani who gives a special gift at Kwanzaa. What do you think the gift might be?

Show pupils the book cover and thumb through the book. Ask pupils to predict what Imani's gift might be and what will happen in the story. Write predictions on the class chart or chalkboard and revisit them after reading the story to check pupils' predictions.

GUIDED READING

Read the story aloud, having pupils read sections aloud as you call upon them. Discuss what happens in the story on each page. Explain any words that pupils do not know.

After reading aloud, have pupils make notes in cooperative learning groups. Give each pupil a copy of the book to read aloud again in their group. Tell them that, as they read each page, the group should discuss it and make notes of what they just learned about Kwanzaa. Have pupils share their notes with the class.

When this part of the activity is completed, instruct pupils to list things they did not learn about Kwanzaa but would like to know. Collect each group's list, and help pupils research their additional questions.

You may wish to have pupils make a class bulletin board showing what they have learned about Kwanzaa.

CROSS CURRICULAR LINKS

LANGUAGE ARTS

Give pupils time to read the additional books and research their Kwanzaa questions.

Encourage pupils to write and illustrate their own Kwanzaa stories. Remind them to include the principles of Nguzo Saba.

Have pupils start a Nguzo Saba journal. Have them write one Nguzo Saba principle on each page and then list how they lived that principle throughout the year.

LANGUAGES: SWAHILI

Swahili words are used to define Kwanzaa symbols, greetings, and principles. Teach children to count, greet, and pronounce symbols and principles of Swahili. Refer to the books listed at the start of this lesson to teach Swahili.

MATHEMATICS

Teach the pupils Swahili numbers, one through ten. Teach pupils to create simple word problems, using Swahili numbers. Give pupils an opportunity to exchange papers and solve the problems, writing their responses in Swahili.

1. moja (mo·jah) means one
2. mbili (m·bee·lee) means two
3. tatu (ta·too) means three
4. nee (n·nay) means four
5. tano (tah·no) means five
6. sita (see·tah) means six
7. saba (sah·bah) means seven
8. nane (nah·nay) means eight
9. tisa (tee·sah) means nine
10. kumi (koo·mee) means ten

ART

Help pupils make Kwanzaa *zawadi* (zuh WAH dee, meaning gifts) to give. African necklaces, masks, and pictures are only a few ideas. Have pupils start by brainstorming their gifts, then listing the materials they will need, collecting them, and making them. Pupils will enjoy exchanging Kwanzaa gifts.

MUSIC

Give pupils time and help in finding and sharing recordings of African music.